SCHOLARS' SLATE PENCILS
COMPO
Smoothest Writing Made in U.S.A. Noiseless
Warranted not to Scratch
COMPO

SHEAFFER
Skrip
®
CARTRIDGE 5-PACK

FOR ALL
SHEAFFER CARTRIDGE
FOUNTAIN PENS

SANDY HOOK, NEW JERSEY

Paolo de Matteis Va. Mus. of Fine Arts

Save Mountain Habitats